This Book Belongs to:

Made in the USA
Las Vegas, NV
17 May 2023

72189974R00069